Department of Health

Third Report of the Committee for Monitoring Agreements on

Tobacco Advertising and Sponsorship

Chairman:
Sir Peter Lazarus, KCB

LONDON: HMSO

© Crown copyright 1990
First published 1990

ISBN 0 11 321306 9

Contents

Chairman: Sir Peter Lazarus KCB
Joint Secretaries: Miss K. Wright
                 Mrs. P. Elcome

Your Reference:
Our Reference

Date:

The Rt Hon Kenneth Clarke QC MP
Secretary of State for Health
Department of Health
Richmond House
79 Whitehall
London SW1A 2NS

9 May 1990

Dear Secretary of State,

In the light of what I said in the forewords to our first two reports, I need add very little this year to the report submitted by the Committee.

The number of complaints made to the Committee, though above last year's total, is still fairly small. I do not find that surprising. Most of those involved with the whole question of cigarette smoking and health are so well aware that the shop front advertisements to which they object as being without health warnings are outside the scope of the Voluntary Agreements that they probably do not take the trouble to bring their complaints to the Committee.

As Chairman of COMATAS, I can only repeat the hope that I have expressed previously, that the negotiations now under way between the Government and the Industry will lead to a speedy resolution of this problem. It is urgently needed if the system of Voluntary Agreements is to retain its credibility.

I should, in all fairness, repeat the point that I have made in my previous forewords, that I am wholly satisfied that the Industry do all they can to comply with the terms of the Agreements. But in conclusion I should express the hope - which I trust will be given due weight during these negotiations - that the Industry will recognise that, after so many years since the system was instituted in agreement with the Government, any cigarette advertisement without a health warning will be regarded as a provocation by all those who believe it to be important that there should be full recognition of the serious health hazards caused by smoking! Any new agreement which does not deal adequately and speedily with that belief will never carry conviction.

Yours sincerely

PETER LAZARUS

The UK Health Ministers
The Minister for Sport
The Tobacco Industry

Third Report of the Committee for Monitoring Agreements on Tobacco Advertising and Sponsorship

1   Introduction

1. The Committee for Monitoring Agreements on Tobacco Advertising and Sponsorship (COMATAS) was set up under the terms of the Voluntary Agreement on Tobacco Products' Advertising and Promotion, and Health Warnings, concluded on 1 April 1986 between HM Government and the United Kingdom tobacco industry as represented by the Tobacco Advisory Council (TAC) and the Imported Tobacco Products Advisory Council (ITPAC). The review date for this agreement was 31 October 1989, and the industry and the Government are currently considering how it should be updated. The existing agreement will continue to operate until it has been revised. The matter is complicated by ongoing discussions on a draft European Community Directive on the Advertising of Tobacco Products in the Press and by means of Bills and Posters.

Terms of reference

2. The Committee's task is to monitor the operation of the aforementioned Agreement on Advertising and the Agreement on Sponsorship of Sport by Tobacco Companies in the United Kingdom which was concluded on 19 January 1987. Summaries of the main provisions of the agreements are to be found in Annex A.

3. The Committee's terms of reference were set out at Appendix 7 to the Agreement on Advertising and are as follows:

"(a) To keep under review all matters relating to the operation of the voluntary agreement other than those relating directly to the operation of the Cigarette Advertising Code and monitored by the Advertising Standards Authority, or matters which are the responsibility of the BBC or the IBA.

(b) To ensure that the terms of the voluntary agreement are properly observed and are interpreted with consistency.

(c) To receive full details of all complaints sent by the public or public bodies to the Government Departments concerned, and of the responses by those companies to whom the complaints were referred. In the case of disputed matters or those which raise general issues relevant to the observance of the agreement, to take a view and, where appropriate, communicate that view to the parties concerned.

(d) To report annually to Ministers, and to member companies through the TAC and ITPAC respectively, on the general implementation of the agreement."

The 1987 Agreement on Sport Sponsorship provided for its provisions to be monitored by the Committee.

Method of working

4. The Committee is required to meet at least quarterly or as often as business demands. Its first meeting was in December 1986 and it has so far met a total of eighteen times, five since the publication of the Second Annual

Report in March 1989. In keeping with the rules set out in the Agreement on Advertising its proceedings are confidential except insofar as its annual report may be published at the discretion of Ministers following consultation with the tobacco industry. The Committee is serviced by a joint secretariat provided by the Government and the Tobacco Advisory Council. After consultation with the tobacco industry, and with the complete agreement of the Committee, both our previous reports have been published.

5. The Committee arranges for the investigation of complaints received. In most cases the relevant company is asked to carry out an investigation and report back to the Committee, although in some cases the secretariat investigates. The Committee than takes a view. The Committee decided at an early stage that to rely solely on the random incidence of complaints as a measure of compliance by the industry would not be sufficient due to the volume and intensity of advertising material in use. Accordingly, in order to provide a more systematic basis for evaluation and in line with its remit, the Committee commissions independent consultants to investigate how certain aspects of the agreements are being adhered to. The Committee has so far commissioned four studies:

(i)   health warnings on shop-front advertising (two studies)

(ii) the location of tobacco posters in relation to schools

(iii) general aspects of two televised sporting events sponsored by tobacco companies.

The results of these studies have been presented in the first two Annual Reports.

Membership

6. The Committee is composed of representatives of the Government departments concerned and the tobacco industry in equal numbers under an independent Chairman appointed with the agreement of Ministers and the Chairman of the Tobacco Advisory Council. As at 1 February 1990 the Committee members were:

Sir Peter Lazarus KCB Chairman

Mr T S Heppell CB DH	Mr W C Owen Tobacco Advisory Council
Mr N M Hale DH	Mr D R Hare Tobacco Advisory Council
Mr W J Burroughs DH	Dr R R Boxall Gallaher Ltd
Mr D A McDonald DoE	Mr E D Oxberry Rothmans (UK) Ltd
Mr A King Scottish Office	Mr A R Haynes Imperial Tobacco Ltd
Mr D Adams Welsh Office	Mr B C W Heard Imported Tobacco Products Advisory Council
Mr J Scott DHSS (NI)	

One place on the industry side of the Committee is temporarily vacant.

Mr A W McCulloch (DH), Mr P A Lee (DoE) and Mr M Goodier (DoE) have attended meetings as observers.

Joint Secretaries

Miss K E Wright DH	Mrs P Elcome Tobacco Advisory Council

7. The Committee thanks the previous Secretaries, Caroline Marijuan and Dudley Backhurst, for their work and welcomes Katherine Wright and Pauline Elcome in their place. They have both served the Committee with great efficiency.

Finances

8. The Committee is funded jointly by the Government and the industry. In the period 1 February 1989 to 31 January 1990 committed expenditure was as follows:

Chairman's fees	£2,000
Telephones, stationery etc	£343.85

Members' and secretaries' expenses were met by their Department or company.

2 Analysis of Responses to Complaints

Sources of Complaints

1. During its third year the Committee received 44 letters of complaint, 16 from private individuals and 28 from organisations (such as health authorities and anti-smoking groups), which contained 168 alleged breaches of the voluntary agreements. This is an increase compared to last year, when the Committee received 28 letters containing 65 alleged breaches of the voluntary agreements.

Nature of Complaints

2. Twenty-nine of the letters received concerned single items only. The other fifteen letters contained multiple complaints, with one letter detailing 64 items. Shop-front advertising was the major cause for complaint, accounting for 119 out of the total 168 alleged breaches. There were eight complaints concerning the agreement on sport sponsorship, over half of which concerned the same subject (a sponsored racing yacht). A quarter of the miscellaneous complaints concerned direct mailing of promotional offers.

Table 2.1 Nature of complaints by number of items

Shop fronts	119
Posters	7
Press/magazines	7
Sport sponsorship	8
Miscellaneous	27
Total	**168**

Committee Conclusions

3. The Committee concluded that twenty of the items complained of were in breach of the agreement and 112 items were not in breach. Nine of the items judged to be in breach of the agreement were defined as inadvertent breaches, where a health warning had been obscured or removed by the actions of a third party for whom the tobacco company could not be held responsible. Thus the item was in breach of the agreement, but the tobacco company was not to blame. Forty-five of the items judged not to be in breach of the agreement were old signs put up before 1983, which do not, therefore, need to carry a health warning. Nine items were considered to be outside the agreements. Two items were referred to the Advertising Standards Authority as they concerned possible breaches of their Cigarette Code, and one was found to be in breach of the ASA Code (the ASA had not come to a decision regarding the other complaint at the time of compiling this report). The Committee was unable to reach a decision on seven items, because when the site was visited the advertisements had already been removed. The Committee was still investigating the remaining 18 items at the time of compiling this report.

Table 2.2 Committee Conclusions

Items in breach	20	
Items not in breach	112	
Outside agreements	9	
Referred to ASA	2	(1 found to breach ASA code)
Unable to reach a conclusion	7	
Still under investigation	18	
Total	**168**	

Young Women's Magazines 4. The following is the list of magazines which should not carry tobacco advertising during 1990 under the terms of the agreement. These figures are the average of the four quarters ending September 1989 based on the National Readership Survey and will stand for the calendar year 1990.

Table 2.3 Young Women's Magazines

Publication	Total Female Readership (000)	% of Female Readership aged 15–24 years
Looks	431	85.77
Mizz	382	83.07
No. 1	243	82.59
Sky	253	81.27
More	301	79.57
Blue Jeans	202	79.52
Just Seventeen	721	78.49
My Guy	306	75.18
'19'	382	72.90
Jackie	369	70.06
Smash Hits	1109	63.16
Clothes Show Mag	600	62.04
Hair and Good Looks	524	58.66
Hair Flair	474	51.72
Elle	701	49.64
Company	423	48.02
New Women	604	41.01
Marie Claire	1116	40.92
Hair	1566	40.44
Wedding and Home	262	38.77
Thoroughbred & Classic Car	232	38.60
Vogue	1265	36.13
Cosmopolitan	1304	35.79
Mother	208	35.17

3 Sport Sponsorship

1. The current Agreement on Sport Sponsorship came into force in January 1987. Its main provisions are set out in Annex A.

2. In the last year, the Committee received eight letters of complaint concerning the sport sponsorship agreement. Six of these letters concerned the same item, a sponsored racing yacht; four of these letters were sent to the Committee in response to press reports during the yacht's construction. The company concerned assured the Committee that the yacht would comply with the sport sponsorship agreement whilst in UK waters. The other complaints were sent to the Committee after the yacht started racing, and the Committee decided that the yacht did, in fact, comply with the terms of the sponsorship agreement. One other item was also found not to breach the agreement, and another was still under investigation at the time this report was compiled.

3. The Committee was also asked to interpret part of the agreement, concerning the placing of advertisements at motor racing tracks. The Committee's conclusion was that there can be no more than four signs per mile of circuit, no matter how many manufacturers and brands are involved. Signs must be a minimum of 440 yards apart, and each sign must not exceed 120 square feet in size.

4. The Agreement requires each tobacco company to notify the Department of the Environment of its plans for sponsorship in the coming year and of any changes to plans. The Department has informed the Committee that this was done in 1989.

4   Financial Aspects of the Agreements

1. There are a number of points in the Agreements which relate to commitments by the industry on financial matters. Figures on expenditure are supplied in confidence to the Department of Health or the Department of the Environment (for sport sponsorship) by the Tobacco Advisory Council and the Imported Tobacco Products Advisory Council. For the first time this year the figures supplied by the Tobacco Advisory Council were certified by an auditor (for details see Chapter 5).

Advertising of lower tar cigarettes

2. The Advertising Agreement says:

"The companies will endeavour to continue to devote a disproportionate amount of advertising to cigarette brands in the two lowest tar groups, as currently defined, in relation to sales in those groups."

(Section 1.3, page 3)

3. The figures for advertising expenditure and market share of the brands in this group for 1988/9 show that, as in previous years, the tobacco industry has not succeeded in this endeavour. The proportion of total advertising expenditure spent on the two lower tar groups does exceed the proportion of the market held by them, but only by an insignificant amount. However, this is due to the fact that these two tar groups now constitute such a large part of the market that to advertise them disproportionately would mean that virtually no advertising would be spent on other brands. The Committee accepts that this is a part of the Agreement which needs to be updated.

4. The figures supplied by the Imported Tobacco Products Advisory Council show that a high proportion of the press and poster advertising was for low tar cigarettes.

Reduction of spending on cigarette brand poster advertising

5. The Advertising Agreement says:

"The companies represented by the Tobacco Advisory Council will limit their expenditure on cigarette brand poster advertising in each successive twelve month period from 1st April 1986 to 50% in aggregate of the level in the year ending 31st March 1980, subject to allowances for inflation as agreed with the DHSS.

The companies represented by the Imported Tobacco Products Advisory Council will ensure that the expenditure on poster advertising of cigarette brands that they import does not exceed 3.5% in aggregate of the limit accepted by the Tobacco Advisory Council for the twelve month period ending 31st March in each year of the Agreement."

(Section 1.4 and 1.5, page 3)

6. The figures from the Tobacco Advisory Council (certified by the auditors) for cigarette brand poster advertising in 1988/89, show that expenditure was within the total permitted spend after making allowances for inflation. The Department of Health has informed the Committee that on the basis of the figures supplied by the Imported Tobacco Products Advisory Council, the amount spent by their members on cigarette brand poster advertising was within the agreed expenditure limit.

Cessation of cinema advertising

7. The Advertising Agreement says:

"There will be no advertising of cigarette brands or hand-rolling tobacco at cinemas after the contracts in force at 1st April 1986 have expired."

(Section 1.6, page 4)

The Tobacco Advisory Council have informed the Department of Health that there has been no advertising in cinemas since the first six months of the Agreement.

Advertising campaign on illegal sales to children under 16

8. The Advertising Agreement says:

"The industry will spend about £1 million p.a. in conducting a campaign with the retail trade at points of retail sale and in the media to encourage support for the law prohibiting the sale of cigarettes to children under 16. Notices on the law will be made extensively available for display by the retail trade and for fixing to automatic vending machines by their operators."

(Section 1.14, page 5)

9. The figure supplied by the Tobacco Advisory Council and certified by audit shows that approximately £1 million was spent in the year ending 31st March 1989.

Sport sponsorship

10. The Agreement on Sport Sponsorship provides for limits for the amount to be spent on the sponsorship of sport in the UK by each individual company in any financial year except after prior consultation with the Minister. The companies make individual returns to the Tobacco Advisory Council, who send the aggregated data to the Department of the Environment. The aggregate data provided by the Tobacco Advisory Council, and certified by audit, show that expenditure on sports sponsorship fell well below the allowed spend using 1985 as a base year and that the proportion of total expenditure spent on media advertising and other promotional material directly related to the events, otherwise than at events, was less than 20%.

5 Independent Investigations Commissioned by the Committee

1. The Committee chose two areas for investigation by independent agents—advertising expenditure and the use of direct mailing promotional offers.

Advertising expenditure

2. Every year the Tobacco Advisory Council supplies the Government in confidence with figures on expenditure on press and poster advertising, sport sponsorship and campaigns to encourage support for the law prohibiting the sale of cigarettes to children under the age of 16. This year, for the first time, these figures were supported by an auditor's certificate.

3. Each company sent their figures, accompanied by a certificate from their auditors, to the Tobacco Advisory Council. These figures were aggregated, and the Tobacco Advisory Council's auditors then certified that the aggregate figure was an accurate sum of the figures from the individual companies. The aggregated figures were then sent to the Department of Health (or the Department of the Environment for sport sponsorship) accompanied by the auditor's certificate.

4. One of the companies was unable to provide exact figures for this year, as it has now ceased to trade in the UK. For this company an estimated figure was accepted.

5. The system of auditing the figures for advertising expenditure will continue in future years.

6. Details of the financial aspects of the agreement are to be found in Chapter 4.

Direct mailing promotional offers

7. During the course of the year the Committee received several complaints about the use of direct mailing promotional offers and decided to investigate this area further. Appendix 4 of the Voluntary Agreement on Tobacco Products' Advertising and Promotion, and Health Warnings contains the provisions which regulate promotional activities, including the use of mailshots.

8. The Committee has decided on the approach to be used, and on the broad outline of a brief for the investigating agents, but some details remained to be decided at the time of compiling this report.

9. The investigation will be carried out by a reputable, independent agent. For example, the management consultancy arm of one of the larger firms of accountants would be suitable. The agent would study direct mail promotions carried out by the tobacco companies, with reference to a set of

criteria decided upon by the Committee. These criteria should enable the agent to assess the extent to which the tobacco company adheres to the provisions of Appendix 4 of the Voluntary Agreement. The agent would then report on the tobacco company's compliance with the Agreement, without revealing commercially sensitive information about the details of the promotions studied.

Voluntary Agreements between the Government and the Tobacco Industry

Agreement on Tobacco Products' Advertising and Promotion, and Health Warnings (agreed in April 1986)

1. Advertising and Promotion

The companies will:

discontinue press and poster advertising of high tar cigarettes;

limit their expenditure per year on cigarette brand poster advertising to 50% of that spent in 1980 in real terms;

discontinue advertising of cigarette brands or hand-rolling tobacco at cinemas, on vehicle exteriors, other than public service vehicles, trams, trolley buses, taxis, and vehicles owned by or contracted to the companies;

endeavour to secure conformity with the requirements of relevant codes of practice whenever advertisers of other products elect to feature illustrations of cigarettes or hand-rolled tobacco packets or branded cigarettes in main media advertisements;

endeavour to ensure that "other goods" bearing tobacco brand names or designs in a manner having the effect of associating the "other goods" with a tobacco product, are not produced for, sold or given away to persons under 18;

spend about £1 million p.a. in conducting a campaign with the retail trade at points of retail sale and in the media to encourage support for the law prohibiting the sale of cigarettes to children under 16;

will not advertise cigarettes or hand-rolling tobacco in video cassettes for sale or hire to the public, or on airships, or balloons or from banner-towing aeroplanes.

2. Schools

There will be no static outdoor cigarette and hand-rolling tobacco brand advertising (excluding signs on retail premises) in close proximity to and clearly visible and identifiable from within buildings or boundaries of schools, places of education or playgrounds predominantly used by young people under 18 years of age, nor adjacent to entrances and exits or the pavements forming boundaries to such schools, places of education and playgrounds.

3. Young Women's magazines

No advertising of cigarettes or hand-rolling tobacco brands will be placed in magazines or periodicals which have a female readership of more than 200,000 and more than 33% of those female readers are aged 15–24.

4. Health Warnings

The companies have agreed to print a new list of health warnings on their product packaging.

The space devoted to health warnings in press and poster advertising will be increased to 17.5% of the area of the advertisement.

New advertising material occupying more than 40 square inches supplied to retailers will carry the appropriate health warnings as soon as possible.

Health warnings should occupy at least 10% of the area of advertisements on retailers' premises or 15% if the tar band is included.

Agreement on Sponsorship of Sport by Tobacco Companies (agreed in January 1987)

1. The agreement sets out more specific controls on tobacco companies' involvement in sponsoring sporting activities, particularly televised sport. Companies will not sponsor sporting activities which appeal mainly to spectators under 18.

Expenditure

2. Overall annual expenditure on sponsorship is reduced to 1985 levels in real terms and for the first time a ceiling, of 20%, is introduced on advertising and promotional activity. Aggregated annual expenditure returns will be submitted to the Department of the Environment who may publish the data.

Health Warnings

3. The agreement provides for the wider use of health warnings. They must, as far as possible, be consistent with those applicable to cigarette advertisements. The size of health warnings at televised events is increased from 10% of total area of the sign to 15%.

Television

4. Television companies have their own codes of practice which, of course, they will continue to apply. Appendix 1 to the new agreement sets out revised controls on static signs at televised sporting activities.

Media Advertising

5. Under the agreement, media advertising must be designed as far as possible not to conflict with the letter and spirit of the Cigarette Code in the British Code of Cigarette Advertising Practice. Advertisements shall not include any representation of a cigarette or a cigarette pack and shall not depict participants in a sport or their equipment.

Printed in the United Kingdom for Her Majesty's Stationery Office
Dd 0292979 C8 6/90